POCKETBOOK
Affirmations

A Book of Affirmations for Women

Alexis,
   I am so excited to support you
in the work this year! I hope
this book provides encouragement
for you as we get deeper into
the work for the good of
students -   Janisha

Tell us how you like this book by leaving a review on Amazon. For other books by this author, visit:

www.kimberlymnesmith.com

For weekly affirmations, follow @CoachKLMN on Instagram and Facebook.

DEDICATED TO...

GOD'S GREATEST CREATION,

Woman.

For all women out there trying to be everything to everyone, this book is for you.

And to all of those special women in my life that keep making me become a better version of myself, each and everyday.

POCKETBOOK
Affirmations

This book is written for all women, trying to do everything for everyone in our lives-the caregiver, the provider, the chef, the housekeeper, and the list goes on and on. You're making it, sometimes barely, sometimes killing the game. But, it's hard for you to remain focused, positive, and sustain your current life. This book has been written for you. The affirmations presented here are to encourage you to keep persevering, but to take time for yourself-to be authentically you.

WHAT ARE AFFIRMATIONS?

Affirmations are positive words or sayings that we say aloud, daily, to combat any negative thoughts or feelings that sometimes come into our brains.

HOW DO I USE THIS BOOK?

This book is a quick reference guide for those daily struggles of life. With an affirmation on each page, you can choose to read the book from start to finish, choose a few affirmations per day to read, or you can flag your favorite affirmations to read daily. The beauty in this book is that it's your choice!

HOW IS THIS BOOK BROKEN DOWN?

There are 10 chapters that have at least 10 affirmations for the chapter topic. For example, if you find yourself needing encouragement with finances, turn to Chapter 2 and work say the affirmations presented there.

TABLE OF

Contents

AFFIRMATIONS OF:

CHAPTER 1

AFFIRMATIONS OF:

Gratitude

I AM
GRATEFUL
FOR
EVERYTHING
GOOD IN MY
WORLD.

THIS WEEK, I WILL SHOW ADDITIONAL GRATITUDE FOR THE PEOPLE I LOVE THROUGH UNEXPECTED ACTS OF KINDNESS.

TODAY, I
START MY DAY
IN GRATITUDE
FOR WHAT I
ALREADY
HAVE AND
ALL OF THE
BLESSINGS
THAT ARE
COMING MY
WAY.

I AM
SATISFIED
WITH WHO I
AM AND
GRATEFUL
FOR WHO I
AM
BECOMING.

DEAR GOD,
THANK YOU...

I AM
GRATEFUL
THAT I AM
ENOUGH.

I AM AN UNSTOPPABLE FORCE FOR GRATITUDE AND GOODNESS.

IN
EVERYTHING, I
GIVE
"THANKS."

I AM
GRATEFUL
FOR THE
BREATH IN MY
BODY.

I AM
THANKFUL
THAT WITH
EACH
EXPERIENCE, I
BECOME A
BETTER
VERSION OF
MYSELF.

CHAPTER 2

AFFIRMATIONS OF:

Finance

I BELIEVE IN MY ABILITY TO USE THE MONEY THAT COMES INTO MY LIFE TO MEET MY FINANCIAL GOALS.

I WILL BE FINANCIALLY FREE.

I AM NOT
POOR, I AM
ON THE PATH
TO A
WEALTHY
LIFE.

I AM A VERY
CAPABLE
PERSON THAT
CAN TACKLE
ALL MONEY
OBSTACLES.

I AM
THANKFUL
FOR MY
CURRENT
FINANCIAL
STATE.

I DESERVE TO
BE PAID FOR
MY TIME,
SKILLS, AND
EFFORTS.

I AM A MONEY MAGNET.

MY TIME AND
MY MONEY
ARE VALUED-I
WILL USE
BOTH OF
THEM WISELY.

I WILL ACCEPT
AND GIVE
UNEXPECTED
FINANCIAL
BLESSINGS.

I WILL USE
MONEY TO
CREATE A
BETTER LIFE
FOR MYSELF
AND MY
FAMILY.

I CONTROL
MONEY,
MONEY WILL
NOT CONTROL
ME.

CHAPTER 3

AFFIRMATIONS OF:

Success

I HAVE
AUTHORITY
AND POWER
TO CHANGE
MY LIFE.

I'M GOING TO
KEEP MY
PROMISES
AND
ACCOMPLISH
MY GOALS.

BECAUSE I
STILL HAVE
BREATH IN MY
BODY, I HAVE
WORK TO DO.

TODAY I WILL
GIVE MY
ABSOLUTE
BEST.

I CAN DO
HARD THINGS.

I HAVE THE
POWER TO
CHANGE MY
LIFE.

TODAY I WILL CHOOSE SUCCESS.

I WILL STRIVE
TO GROW,
EXPAND, AND
SEE MY
BUSINESS OR
CAREER
THRIVE.

I HAVE WHAT
IT TAKES TO
REACH MY
GOALS.

I HAVE THE
ABILITIES AND
TOOLS TO
ACCOMPLISH
EVERY GOAL I
SET.

MY
POTENTIAL TO
CONQUER
ANY AND ALL
CHALLENGES
ARE
LIMITLESS.

MY ABILITY
TO SUCCEED
IS INFINITE.

I AM A
DREAMER,
AND MY
DREAMS WILL
COME TRUE.

CHAPTER 4

AFFIRMATIONS OF:

Happiness

HAPPINESS
AND
GRATITUDE
COME EASY
FOR ME.

TODAY, I
CHOOSE
HAPPINESS.

HAPPINESS IS
MY
BIRTHRIGHT.

I DESERVE TO
BE HAPPY AND
FEEL GOOD.

TODAY AND
EVERYDAY, I
WILL ENJOY
LIVING IN THE
PRESENT
MOMENT.

MY HAPPINESS
WILL
INCREASE
DAILY.

I AM
BECOMING A
BETTER
VERSION OF
MYSELF DAY
BY DAY.

TODAY I
CELEBRATE
WHO I AM
AND THE
PERSON I'M
BECOMING.

MY HOME IS A
HAPPY PLACE.

HAPPINESS,
JOY, SUCCESS,
AND AN
ABUNDANT
LIFE ALL
BELONG TO
ME.

CHAPTER 5

AFFIRMATIONS OF:

Love

I AM KIND
HEARTED, I'M
HERE TO
LOVE.

I AM A
LOVING
POWERFUL
FORCE IN
THIS WORLD.

I REFUSE TO
FEEL GUILTY
FOR LOVING
MYSELF.

I DESERVE GOOD THINGS IN LIFE.

ALL MY
RELATIONSHIPS
ARE HAPPY AND
HEALTHY.

MY PARTNER IS
A REFLECTION
OF ME.

MY HEART IS
OPEN FOR NEW
LOVE AND
CONNECTIONS.

I CHOOSE TO
BRING LOVE
INTO
SITUATIONS I
ENCOUNTER
TODAY.

I AM GRATEFUL
FOR THE
PEOPLE WHO
LOVE ME IN MY
LIFE.

I WILL NOT
APOLOGIZE
FOR BEING
MYSELF.

CHAPTER 6

AFFIRMATIONS OF:

Health & Fitness

I WILL ALLOW
TIME FOR MY
BODY TO
REST.

TODAY I WILL
MAKE
HEALTHY
FOOD
CHOICES.

I AM KIND TO
MY BODY AND
CHOOSE NOT
TO CHANGE IT
FOR ANYBODY
BUT MYSELF.

I WILL HAVE A PRODUCTIVE WORKOUT TODAY.

MY BODY
WILL BECOME
STRONGER.

I CHOOSE THE
BEST THINGS
TO PUT IN MY
BODY.

I AM SAFE IN
MY SKIN.

I HONOR MY
BODY BY
TRUSTING THE
SIGNALS IT
SENDS ME.

TODAY I WILL
PROTECT MY
PEACE.

I AM HAPPY,
HEALTHY,
CONTENT,
AND
PROSPEROUS.

CHAPTER 7

AFFIRMATIONS OF:

Positive thinking

TODAY IS
GOING TO BE
A GREAT DAY.

EVEN IN MY DARKEST MOMENTS, I WILL REMAIN OPTIMISTIC.

TODAY, I WILL
SEIZE THE
DAY WITH
POSITIVE
ENERGY, A
RENEWED
MIND, AND
FRESH EYES.

I AM THE CREATOR OF MY FUTURE.

DELAYS ARE
AN
OPPORTUNITY
TO REFLECT.

I SURROUND
MYSELF WITH
PEOPLE WHO
EXUDE
POSITIVE
ENERGY TO
LIFT ME UP
AND BRING
PURPOSE INTO
MY LIFE.

I AM THE
ARCHITECT OF
MY LIFE.

I AM FOCUSED ON THOUGHTS THAT EMPOWER ME AND RELEASE THOUGHTS THAT DRAIN ME.

I DO NOT
BELIEVE IN
REJECTIONS, I
BELIEVE IN
REDIRECTION.

I WILL
RADIATE
POSITIVE
ENERGY TO
THOSE I
ENCOUNTER.

I AM AWARE
THAT
EVERYTHING
IS HAPPENING
FOR ME, NOT
TO ME.

CHAPTER 8

AFFIRMATIONS OF:

Abundance

I WELCOME
POSITIVE
VIBES,
KINDNESS,
AND
ABUNDANT
LOVE INTO
MY LIFE.

I SET AND LIVE
UP TO HIGH
EXPECTATIONS
IN MY LIFE.

I AM
ABUNDANTLY
BLESSED.

TODAY I
WELCOME ALL
ABUNDANCE
AND
PROSPERITY.

I DESERVE A
PROSPEROUS
LIFE.

I HAVE THE
POTENTIAL TO
MANIFEST MY
DREAMS INTO
REALITY.

TODAY I WILL
BEGIN TO USE
THE TALENTS
I'VE BEEN
GIFTED.

I AM OPEN TO RECEIVE.

I HAVE MORE THAN ENOUGH.

MY DREAMS
ARE WORTHY
OF MY
TALENT.

CHAPTER 9

AFFIRMATIONS OF:

Self-Esteem

I AM THE BEST
VERSION OF
ME-THE
PERSON I AM
AND THE
PERSON I AM
BECOMING.

TODAY, I
FORGIVE
MYSELF FOR
MY MISTAKES
AND WILL
PRESS
FORWARD.

I AM
COURAGEOUS,
INTELLIGENT,
AND HAVE
VALUE.

I AM WHO I
AM, THERE'S
NO ONE LIKE
ME.

I AM TOO BIG
A GIFT TO THE
WORLD TO
WASTE TIME.

WHEN LIFE
GETS TOUGH, I
WILL KEEP
TRYING.

I AM
COUNTING ON
MYSELF
BECAUSE
OTHERS ARE
DEPENDING
ON ME.

I CHOOSE TO
FEEL GOOD
ABOUT
MYSELF.

I WILL
FORGIVE
THOSE WHO
HAVE HARMED
ME IN THE
PAST.

GRACE IS
SUFFICIENT.
TODAY I WILL
ACCEPT
GRACE.

I CAN DO ANYTHING I PUT MY MIND TO.

CHAPTER 10

AFFIRMATIONS OF:

I Am

I AM ENOUGH.

I AM CAPABLE.

I AM
BRILLIANT.

I AM
LIMITLESS.

I AM LOVED.

I AM
GRATEFUL.

I AM
RESILIENT
AND CAN GET
THROUGH
ANYTHING.

I AM
BECOMING
WHO I AM
DESTINED TO
BE.

I AM HAPPY.

I AM PROUD.

I AM
HEALTHY.

I AM
SUPPORTED.

I AM
CONFIDENT.

I AM
RADIANTLY
BEAUTIFUL.

I AM
UNSTOPPABLE.

Made in United States
Orlando, FL
05 October 2022

23019740R00070